A Theory of the Theater

PUBLICATIONS

of the

Dramatic Museum

OF COLUMBIA UNIVERSITY

IN THE CITY OF NEW YORK

Third Series

Papers on Playmaking :

I HOW SHAKSPERE CAME TO WRITE THE 'TEMPEST'. By Rudyard Kipling. With an introduction by Ashley H. Thorndike.

II HOW PLAYS ARE WRITTEN. Letters from Augier, Dumas, Sardou, Zola and others. Translated by Dudley Miles. With an introduction by William Gillette.

III A STAGE PLAY. By Sir William Schenck Gilbert. With an introduction by William Archer.

IV A THEORY OF THE THEATER. By Francisque Sarcey. Translated by H. H. Hughes. With an introduction and notes by Brander Matthews.

V (Extra volume) A catalog of Models and of Stage-Sets in the Dramatic Museum of Columbia University.

PAPERS ON PLAYMAKING

IV

A Theory of the Theater

BY

FRANCISQUE SARCEY

WITH AN INTRODUCTION BY

BRANDER MATTHEWS

Printed for the

Dramatic Museum of Columbia University
in the City of New York
MCMXVI

CONTENTS

INTRODUCTION

IN the brilliant essay on the Comédie-Française which Henry James wrote forty years ago, and which had for its text the series of critical analyses of the histrionic attainments of the chief performers at the House of Molière, then recently put forth by Francisque Sarcey, the American critic declared that the French critic was so predominant in the Parisian press that he held "in his hand the fortune of a play" and that if he "devoted an encouraging line and a half to a young actress, mademoiselle immediately had a career." This may be an overstatement, but it can hardly be called a misstatement. For the final thirty years of the nineteenth century Sarcey was the most influential of all the theatrical reviewers of France, even if he could not actually make or unmake a new play or a new player.

Henry James analized the reasons for Sarcey's enviable influence and for the weight of his words. Sarcey was "sternly incorruptible;" he had "a religious respect for his theme;" he had a habit of taking the theater seriously, with "unwearying attention to detail;" he had "the scenic sense, the theatrical eye;" he was "shrewd and sagacious, and almost tiresomely in earnest." And now that nearly a score of years have past since Sarcey ceased to contribute to the *Temps* his weekly review of the passing show, a later generation has ratified the praise, even if not a few latterday critics are disposed to see Sarcey's limitations with a disenchanted eye. M. Gustave Lanson, for example, in his inestimable history of French literature, holds that Sarcey's theory of the theater was somewhat too narrow and that it was sometimes too rigidly enforced.

But no one of the younger generation has denied that Sarcey had a theory of the theater, that this theory has left its impress upon the contemporary French drama, and that it had been developed by Sarcey himself as the immediate consequence of his immense experience and of his indefatigable attendance in the playhouse. Sarcey's opinions about the art of the drama were the direct result of his observations in the theater itself,—just as were the opinions of Aristotle and of Lessing.

2

He had no kinship with the erudite Italian theorists of the Renascence who evolved their dramatic dogmas from their inner consciousness, being deprived of the privilege of persistent playgoing and having occasion only sporadically to see a good play well acted.

Sarcey was continually seeing good plays well acted; he was continually analizing his own impressions at these performances, and he was continually investigating the impressions made upon his fellow-playgoers. As a result of this relentless inquiry, pursued for two score years, he discovered for himself certain of the principles of the drama,—just as Lessing had discovered them in like manner a century earlier. For Lessing, Sarcey had ever an exalted respect, as a critic of the keenest acumen and as a constant playgoer of alert intelligence. He said to me once that when he chanced to find in Lessing's 'Hamburg Dramaturgy' an opinion which he had already arrived at by his own reflexion, he felt encouraged and confirmed in his belief that his own view was sound.

When we compare Sarcey as a dramatic critic with a predecessor like Jules Janin or with a contemporary like Jules Lemaitre we cannot help noting that however inferior he may be in wit, in felicity of phrase, in charm of style, he is superior in his possession of a compact body of doctrine about the drama, which might be a little too systematic at times, but which sustained and supported his judgments upon the plays of the moment and which gave to these judgments a validity and a significance often absent from the sparkling effusions of Janin and Lemaitre, neither of whom took the theater very seriously and both of whom now and then yielded to the temptation of accepting the play they were supposed to be criticizing either as a peg on which to hang pretty garlands of figures of speech or as a springboard from which to dive off into philosophical disquisition.

Sarcey might on occasion apply his code too rigorously; but at least he had a code to apply. He might be over-emphatic at times in declaring the rigid limits of the drama and in insisting upon the futility of well meant efforts to enlarge its scope, to broaden its mission, to bestow upon it a more significant message; but he was inexorably honest in setting forth these opinions of his, and they were founded upon an intimacy with the theater possest by none of his opponents. As to his critical insight and his integrity there is no room for dispute; and not a few of the principles Sarcey insisted upon, either first declared by him or by him more clearly formulated, are now among the commonplaces of dramatic criticism, employed incessantly by writers often unfamiliar with his name.

In his weekly articles Sarcey frequently mentioned the book which he proposed to devote to the 'History of Theatrical Conventions'; but he never wrote it,—and perhaps he never really intended to write it. Thirty years ago when I askt him when this long awaited volume was to appear, he laught and responded, "If I ever do write it, what shall I have left to fill up those long columns of my weekly article in the *Temps?*" Yet he had at least made a beginning of this book in a series of more or less connected articles publisht weekly in the *Temps* in the summer and fall of 1876, when there happened to be only a few new plays demanding critical consideration.

After Sarcey's death in May, 1899, there was an immediate demand for a collection of his theatrical reviews. This demand had been heard during his lifetime and he had always resisted it, on the ground that his articles contributed to a daily paper and dealing with the plays of the day, were too journalistic in tone and in temper, too temporary in their illustrations and allusions, to warrant their reproduction in a series of volumes aspiring to the dignity and permanence of literature. Other Parisian dramatic reviewers, Jules Janin and Théophile Gautier, Auguste Vitu and Jules Lemaitre, might garner their newspaper sheaves and strive to rescue their hebdomadal effusions from the swift oblivion of the back number; but Sarcey resolutely refused to be tempted by the lure of this fleeting immortality.

What he had declined to do himself his son-in-law, Adolphe Brisson, piously undertook after his death; and in 1900 Brisson issued the first volume of 'Quarante ans de Théatre,' followed in rapid succession by six other volumes, in which selections from Sarcey's weekly articles were classified under various heads. The first volume dealt with the Comédie-Française, always the center of Sarcey's solicitude; and it contained also his discussion of the principles of dramatic criti-

cism.   More valuable than this discussion
was the group of successive articles written
in 1876 in which he considered the funda-
mental basis of the art of the theater, in
which he dealt with the necessity of conventions in the drama (as in all the other arts),
and in which he discust the separation of
species, the setting off of the tragic from the
comic.

It is a selection from this series of papers
which is here translated, with many excisions
and suppressions, due to the desire to present
Sarcey's views in a form easy of apprehension
by readers not so familiar with the French
stage as were the subscribers to the *Temps*
forty years ago.   The excisions have been
made so as to sharpen Sarcey's points without
in any way modifying or obscuring his views;
and the passages selected for presentation
here adequately reveal his method, which was
closely akin to the method of Aristotle and
to the method of Lessing.   They disclose
also his manner, his intellectual integrity, his
playful common sense, his total absence of
pedantic pretentiousness.

This inquiry into the esthetic of the theater
seems to be only a portico to an edifice which

was never erected; and yet even if it is but a beginning, it sets forth sound doctrine about the drama. It contains at least the outline of his opinions in regard to theatrical conventions; and it is greatly to be regretted that he never resumed the articles and that he never supported these opinions by the host of illustrations he employed in later years in dealing with the drama of the day.

Perhaps it may be well here to supplement the condensed statement of the necessary conventions of the drama which Sarcey made in the articles in the *Temps* from which these selections have been taken, and to amplify the theory he laid down. He began by declaring that the drama, like all the other arts exists and can exist only by departing from the mere facts; and he had no difficulty in showing that the painter is also forced to express the essential truth of nature by suppressing or altering reality. The late John La Farge, in his very suggestive essay on 'Ruskin, Art and Truth,' made a similar declaration of principles:—

"When I work as an artist I begin at once by discarding the way in which things are really done, and by translating them at once

8

into another material. Therein consists the pleasure that you and I take in the work of art,—perhaps a new creation between us. The pleasure that such and such reality gives me and you has been transposed. The great depth and perspective of the world, its motion, its never resting, I have arrested and stopt upon a little piece of flat paper. That very fact implies that I consider the flatness of my paper a fair method of translating the non-existence of *any* flatness in the world that I look at. If I am a sculptor I make for you this soft, moving, fluctuating, colored flesh in an immovable hard, rigid, colorless material; and it is this transposition which delights you, as well as me in a lesser degree who have made it. Therefore at the very outset of my beginning to affect you by what is called the record of a truth, I am obliged to ask you to accept a number of the greatest impossibilities, evident to the senses, and sometimes disturbing when the convention supposed to be agreed upon between you and myself is understood by only one of the two parties in the carrying out of the matter."

In other words, the art of the painter is possible only when there is a convention, an implied contract, between the artist and his public, that he can translate and transpose in contradiction to the facts, and that he is permitted to represent as motionless (for the chosen moment) that which is in reality never still. So the art of the sculptor is based on a tacit agreement, which permits him to represent in clay or marble or bronze, in hard monochrome, that which in fact is soft and multicolored. So the art of the drama is possible only when the convention is accepted that the playwright may condense his story and omit all the needless details and all the extraneous particularities which would in real life delay and dilute the action.

The dramatist has to accept the condition that his plays are to be performed, by actors, in a theater and before an audience. The actor departs from the fact, and must so depart, when he makes love in tones that reach clearly to the last row of seats in the topmost gallery. The theater can present a forest with growing trees only by the aid of painted canvas, which we must accept in accordance with our agreement. And the audience has only a limited time and a limited understanding, so that the story must move swiftly and must be made transparently clear by artifices of exposition.

The convention underlying the modern problem-play in prose is that all the characters say what they have to say in the fewest possible words and that what they say is understood by all the other characters at the first hearing. The convention underlying the comedy of Molière is that all the characters belong to a race of beings, whose native and necessary speech is the rimed French alexandrine. In Shaksperian tragedy this native and necessary speech is English blank verse. In pantomime it is gesture; and in opera it is song.

When Tolstoy, in his misguided attempt to ascertain 'What is Art' objected to a dying tenor in silk tights singing with his last breath, he was simply refusing to be a party to the convention by which alone can opera exist. This refusal was of course within Tolstoy's right; but by it he deprived himself of the specific pleasure which only the art of the modern music-drama can bestow.

In all the forms of the drama, comedy and tragedy, problem-play, pantomime and opera, the audience gladly permits departures from the facts of life, if this departure is for its pleasure and for its profit. In reality Othello and Desdemona talkt to each other in Italian, yet as few of us are familiar with any tongue but our own, we are glad to have them speak English. But if we wish to enjoy a performance by two great actors of different races, Othello by Salvini and Iago by Booth, we must extend the license we have granted by our implied contract and permit Othello to use the language which he would have used in real life while Iago and all the others to use the language which they would not have used but which is more satisfactory to us.

Probably this theory of the conventions by which alone the drama is made possible had been suggested by one or another of Sarcey's predecessors,—altho I have failed to find anything of the kind in all my reading in the history of theatrical theory. Even if suggested by one or another of the earlier critics, the theory owes its general acceptance today to the sharpness with which Sarcey seized it, to the clearness with which he set it forth, and to the frequency with which he insisted on it.

Another theory of Sarcey's, not so important, perhaps, and yet as useful, is that which asserts that there are in every story suitable for the stage certain interviews, certain moments, certain scenes, which the dramatist must show us in action, which he cannot merely relate, and which must not happen between the acts. Sarcey called these the *scenès à faire*, the scenes which must be dealt with by the dramatist, and which can be omitted only at the risk of dumbly disappointing the spectators. Mr. William Archer has accepted this theory, and has suggested that we should term the *scènes à faire*, the Obligatory Scenes.

Unfortunately M. Brisson has not replevined for us any one of Sarcey's articles in which this theory is stated. Therefore it has seemed best to devote the second half of these selections to Sarcey's characteristically logical discussion of the artistic advisability of separating the comic and the tragic. Even if Sarcey's argument is not altogether convincing to us of the Anglo-Saxon tradition, it is one which it is wise for us to consider carefully and to weigh cautiously. Attention should also be called to the fact that altho Sarcey was here setting forth a dogma strenuously insisted upon by the Italian promulgators of the classicist code, he did not support it by the argument they derived from their study of Greek and Latin drama, in which they discovered that there were no humorous passages in tragedy and no strongly dramatic passages in comedy. Sarcey was consistent in basing his contention upon his analysis of the attitude of the audience, on his observation of the difficulty experienced by Parisian playgoers when they were confronted by the necessity of changing abruptly from the mood of tears to the mood of laughter.

BRANDER MATTHEWS.

(April, 1916.)

A Theory of the Theater

A Theory of the Theater

I.

I AM going to propose for your consideration the ideas which I believe should form the first chapter of a treatise on the art of the theater. But a few words by way of preface are necessary. Most readers, when you speak to them of a treatise on the art of the theater, or to express it more simply as did our fathers, when you speak to them of the Rules of dramatic art, believe that you have in mind a code of precepts by the aid of which one is assured, if he writes, oᶠ composing a piece without faults, or if he criticizes, of being able to place his finger precisely on every defect.

At bottom this prepossession is entirely French; and it does not date from yesterday. You doubtless recall the worthy Abbé d'Aubignac who, having promulgated a code of dramatic literature, wrote a tragedy according to his own formula and made it prodigously tiresome. This misadventure has never cured the public of its belief in the efficacy of Rules.

They were cited against Corneille when he wrote the 'Cid,' and against Molière when he gave us the 'School for Wives.' Poor Corneille struggled as best he could in his prefaces to release himself from these laws which threatened to strangle him. And in the 'Critique de l'École des Femmes' Molière has preserved for us a record of the annoyances which the pedants of his time sought to impose on him; and it is here that he delivered his famous dictum: "There is no other Rule of the theater than that of pleasing the public."

We have laught at this overstatement; we have not taken it at all seriously; and less than sixty years ago our fathers saw what difficulty those who were then called the Romanticists experienced in freeing themselves from the fetters of the code of tragedy laid down by Bossu, put into verse by Boileau, commented upon and reinforced by all the critics of the eighteenth century, with Voltaire at their head and after him La Harpe and Marmontel.

This national prejudice has its root in our

philosophic education. From our infancy we have been taught that there is an ideal perfection which has an existence of its own and which is like an emanation from divinity; that everybody carries about with him a conception of it more or less clear, an image more or less enfeebled; and that works of art should be declared good or bad according as they approach or depart from this type of perfection.

I will not entangle myself by affirming that there is no such beau ideal or archetype of absolute perfection. I confess simply that I do not know what is meant by this, that these are questions outside my province, which I do not comprehend. It may be that in the sublunary regions there exists a form of drama supreme and marvellously perfect of which our masterpieces are only pale counterfeits; I leave to those who have had the good fortune of beholding this, and who say they are delighted by it, the duty and the pleasure of speaking of it with competence.

Rules do not render any great service in criticizing any more than they do in creating. The best that can be said for them is that they may serve as directions or guide-posts.

After all, those who have no ear never love music and always beat time out of measure when they listen. Native taste sustained and purified by training, reflexion, and usage, can alone help you to enjoy works of art. The first condition of having pleasure is to love; and we do not love by rule.

It is customary in seeking.a definition of dramatic art to say that drama is the representation of life. Now, assuredly drama is the representation of life. But when one has said that, he has said no great thing; and he has taught nothing to those whom he has furnisht with this formula.

All the arts of imitation are representations of life. All have for their purpose the placing of nature before our eyes. What other object has painting than that of portraying for us either scenes from life or places which serve as a setting for it? And does not sculpture strive to render for us the images of living creatures, now single and now joined in groups. We may say with equal truth of all the arts that they are representations of life; in other words, copies from nature. But we see just as readily (for it is an observation that does not require reflexion) that each of these arts has a different means of expression, that the conditions to which it is obliged to submit in order to represent life impose on each of them the employment of particular processes. Thus painting concerns itself with the representation on a plane surface of objects which have all their dimensions and of scenes from life which in reality would require for their existence a vast depth of background. It is clear that if you wish to suggest a theory of painting you must take careful account of this condition and of all the others, if there are any others, which are essential to this art, without which the art itself could not exist.

The first question to be settled then is that of the conditions, material or moral, in which resides necessarily and inevitably the art of which we speak. As it is impossible to separate the art from these conditions, as it lives only thru and by them, as it is not a subtle inspiration wafted from heaven or emanating from the depths of the human mind, but something wholly concrete and definite which, like all living things, cannot exist except in the environment to which it is adapted, we are moved naturally to analize this environment to which the art has accommodated its life, from which it has sprung, so to speak, by a series of successive developments, and of which it will always retain the impress. The painter takes a bit of wood or a scrap of canvas on which to represent life. It is a plane surface, is it not? Here is a fact, sure, undeniable. We will set out from there.

In the same way let us inquire concerning dramatic art if there is not also a fact which corresponds to this fact in painting and which is in like manner the indispensable condition of its existence and development. If we find this fact we shall be able to draw logically some conclusions as incontestable as the fact itself; and we shall discover afterwards the proof of these conclusions in the history of the art.

Now, in regard to the theater there is one fact which cannot fail to strike the least attentive; it is the presence of an audience. The word play carries with it the idea of an audience. We cannot conceive of a play without an audience. Take one after another the accessories which serve in the performance of a dramatic work—they can all be replaced or suppressed except that one. Thus theaters ordinarily are provided with a platform in the form of a stage, but you can imagine one without this; in fact comedies are played in drawing-rooms without changing the arrangement of the room. This may not be very convenient, but at any rate it does not alter the meaning of the comedy. The foot-lights are arranged to light the actors from below; and this is a very useful device, since it places the faces of the actors in full light and makes them seem younger and more animated by suppressing the shadows of the eyebrows and the nose. But is it a necessary condition? Assuredly not. You may imagine such other lighting system as you please, to say nothing of the sun, which was the sole illumination of the ancients who certainly had a theater. You may even dispense with the scenery and the costumes. Corneille and Molière have been played in barns by strolling actors grotesquely costumed according to the state of their humble wardrobes. It was none the less the 'Cid' or the 'School for Wives.' Shakspere, as we have been told a hundred times, did not trouble himself in the least about scenery. A board was set up on the stage which indicated in writing where the action was taking place; and the imagination of the spectator filled in the rest to suit himself. It was none the less 'Othello' or 'Romeo and Juliet.'

But a play without an audience is inconceivable. It is possible that a king may at some time or other indulge the fantasy of seating himself alone in a play-house and having played for himself alone some piece commanded by him. Such an eccentricity is only the exception which proves the rule. The king represents the absent audience; he is the crowd all by himself. And likewise the famous solitary spectator at the Odéon in the old days—the one whom Lireux provided with a foot-warmer,—he was the representative of the absent multitude. This legendary spectator was not only a spectator, he was the public. He included in his own person the twelve hundred truants who should have occupied the vacant seats about him. They had delegated their powers to him; it was they who applauded with his hands and who bore witness of their boredom when he opened his mouth to yawn.

It is an indisputable fact that a dramatic work, whatever it may be, is designed to be listened to by a number of persons united and forming an audience, that this is its very essence, that this is a necessary condition of its existence. As far back as you can go in the history of the theater, in all countries and in all ages, the men who have ventured to give a representation of life in dramatic form having begun by gathering the spectators, Thespis around his chariot as Dumas around his 'Étrangère.' It is with a public in view that they have composed their works and had them performed. This then we can insist on:—No audience no play. The audience is the necessary and inevitable condition to which dramatic art must accommodate its means.

II.

I emphasize this point because it is the point of departure, because from this simple fact we can derive all the laws of the theater without a single exception.

A moment ago I said that the painter is constantly obliged to represent everything on a flat surface, whether objects having all their dimensions or deep perspectives. How does he accomplish this? By a series of conventions, or tricks if you prefer, some of which are indicated and imposed by the structure and habit of our eyes and can hardly be modified, while the others are mere traditions which have no foundation in the necessity of things and are constantly variable. The same is true of the theater. Its business is to represent life to a crowd. This crowd performs in some sort for dramatic art the function of the flat surface in painting. It requires the intervention of similar tricks, or if you like the term better, of conventions. An example or two in order to enable you better to understand this. A crowd can scarcely be held together for more than four hours; or put it at five, six, eight, ten—let us say a whole day, tho that is going rather far. It is certain that the following day, if this crowd collects again, it will not be composed of the same elements. It will still be a crowd, but it will not be the same crowd. The representation of life that we can exhibit before a crowd cannot then exceed an average of six hours in length. That is a fact of absolute necessity, against which no argument can prevail. The reading of a book may continue two months, the reader remaining always the same. But the crowd, by the fact of being a crowd, requires that a drama end in six hours or less.

The action represented evidently lasts more than six hours. Even in case it were confined within this narrow limit (which might happen after all) it would require a mass of innumerable details for which we could find no room under this compression of time. It was necessary a moment ago to resort to deceptions in order to represent perspective on a flat surface; it will be necessary to resort to conventions in order to give the impression that a long time has elapst when we have only six hours at our disposal.

Let us take another example, drawn this time from the moral order. It is asserted that a crowd thinks and feels differently from the individuals which compose it. I do not imagine that there is need at present of proving a fact so well known and so authentic.

The distinguishing mark then of this collective being which we call the public is a certain confirmation of the eye. It has the singular privilege of seeing things from another angle, illuminated by a light different from that of reality. The crowd changes the appearance of these things; where there are certain lines it sees others; where there are colors of a certain sort it sees different shades.

Well, if you present to this collective being, whose eyes have this gift of bizarre transformation, events from life just as they happen in reality, they will strike the crowd as being false, for they appear to the spectators altogether different from what they appear to the individuals composing the audience.

Suppose a scene-painter should give to his canvas backgrounds the tones he has observed in nature, his picture, lighted by the glare of the foot-lights, would appear grotesque. So do facts and sentiments drawn from reality and transported just as they are to the stage. It is absolutely necessary to accommodate them to the particular disposition of mind which results among people when they assemble in the form of a crowd, when they compose an audience. Therefore deceptions —conventions—are essential. Among these conventions some are permanent, others temporary and changeable. The reason is easy to understand. The audience is composed of individuals; and among individuals there are sentiments—in very small number, it is true,—which are general and universal, which we find in varying degrees among all the civilized peoples who alone have developed a dramatic art. Likewise there are prejudices (in still smaller number) which we encounter in all times and in all countries. These sentiments, these prejudices, or in a word, these ways of looking at things, always remaining the same, it is natural that certain conventions, certain tricks, should be inherent in all drama, and that they should be establisht as laws.

On the contrary there are other sentiments, other prejudices, which are changeable, which vanish every time one civilization is succeeded by another, and which are replaced by different ways of seeing.

When the eyes of the audience change, the conventions invented to give the illusion of life should change also, and the laws which the technic each epoch has promulgated and which it has in good faith believed to be universal and unchangeable are destined to fall. But these laws may hold good for a long time; and they do not crumble except under the repeated assaults of intelligent criticism and of innovators of genius.

What are the universal conventions, those that have their root in all humanity? What, on the other hand, are the temporary conventions? What has been their influence? How have they arisen and how fallen into disuse?

It is not sufficient simply to affirm that drama is the representation of life. It would be a more exact definition to say that dramatic art is the sum total of the conventions, universal or local, permanent or temporary, by the aid of which in representing life in the theater, the audience is given the illusion of truth.

III.

Man, by the fact of being man, in all countries and in all ages, has had the privilege of expressing his joy or his grief by laughter or by tears. There are other animals that weep, but of all the beings of creation man is the only one that laughs. Why does he laugh? And what are the causes of laughter? It is not necessary for the moment to answer this question. Man laughs; this is a fact which cannot be disputed. He weeps; that is evident. He does not laugh nor does he weep in the same fashion or at the same things in company as alone. A crowd laughs more heartily and boisterously than an individual. Tears are readier and more abundant with an audience than with a single man.

From this disposition of the public to express the most universal sentiments of human nature, of joy and of sorrow, by laughter and by tears, arises the great division of the drama into plays that are cheerful and plays that are sad; into comedy with all its subspecies, and into tragedy and drama with all their varieties.

I do not say that it is the mission of the dramatic author to bring life as it actually is on the stage; that as there are in real life events, some pleasant and some unpleasant, it necessarily follows that we must have comedies and tragedies.

I hold that reality, if presented on the stage truthfully, would appear false to the monster with the thousand heads which we call the public. We have defined dramatic art as the sum total of the conventions by the aid which, in the theater, we represent life and give to the twelve hundred people assembled the illusion of truth.

In themselves, events are not cheerful and they are not sad. They are neither. It is we who impregnate them with our sentiment or color them to our liking. An old man falls; the street urchin who is passing holds his sides and laughs. The woman cries out with pity. It is the same event; but the one has thought only of the ridiculousness of the fall, the other has seen only the danger. The second wept where the first found cause only for laughter.

It is with events from human life as it is with landscapes. We often say of one view that it is hideous and of another that it is agreeable. This is an abuse of words. It is we who bestow on the places we pass the sentiments that move us; it is our imagination which transforms them; and it is we who give them a soul—our own.

It is true that certain landscapes seem better adapted to harmonize with the grief of a heart which is sad; but imagine two lovers in the most forbidding spot, in the midst of steep cliffs, surrounded by dark forests and stagnant waters. The spot would be illumined for them by their love and would remain graven in their memory in delightful outlines. This perfect indifference of nature has even become in recent times a commonplace of poetic development. There is nothing which has more inspired our poets; everybody remembers the two admirable tunes in which Victor Hugo and Alfred de Musset played upon this theme: 'Tristesse d' Olympio' and 'Souvenir.'

How often may we not observe in actual life that which has been pointed out to us in a well-known example in the classic repertory; viz., that the same situation may be treated by laughter or by tears, transported from the comic to the tragic. Mithridates wishes to know of Monime whether in his absence Xiphares has not made love to her, whether she does not love the young man. In order to make her tell the truth he pretends to believe himself too old for her and offers to marry her to the son who will be better able to take his place in her affection. Monime allows the fatal confession to escape and everybody shivers at the famous line:

"Sire, you change countenance."

Harpagon, in the 'Miser' of Molière, uses the same artifice with Cléante; and the whole audience laughs at the rage of the old man

when he delivers his malediction to his son
who does not wish to surrender Marianne.
It is not then with events, matter inert and
indifferent, that we should concern ourselves,
but with the public which laughs or weeps
according as certain chords are toucht in
preference to others.

Having establisht this point we shall
answer easily a question which has caused the
spilling of a great deal of ink and which has
been greatly obscured because those who
have discust it have not sought out the fun-
damental principles.

We agreed just now that by a very natural
classification plays are divided into comedies
and tragedies. May we have, is it well that
we have, pieces for the stage in which laughter is mingled with tears, in which comic
scenes succeed painful situations?

Most of those who rebel against the sustained seriousness of tragedy, who advocate
the mixing of the tragic and the comic in the
same play, have set out with the idea that
it is thus things happen in reality and that
the art of the dramatist consists in **transporting** reality to the stage. It is this very
simple view that Victor Hugo sets forth in

his admirable preface to 'Cromwell' in that highly imaginative style which is so characteristic of him. I prefer to quote this brilliant passage:

"In drama, as one may conceive it, even tho he is unable to write it, everything is linkt together and everything follows in sequence as in real life. The body here plays a part as the soul does; and men and events set in action by this double agent pass before us ludicrous and terrible by turns, sometimes terrible and ludicrous at the same time.

Thus the judge will say: 'Off with his head,—let's to dinner.' Thus the Roman Senate will deliberate on the turbot of Domitian. Thus Socrates, drinking the hemlock and discoursing of the immortality of the soul and the one god, pauses to recommend that a cock be sacrificed to Esculapius. Thus Elizabeth swears and speaks Latin.

Thus Richelieu will be companioned by the monk Joseph, and Louis XI will be escorted by his barber, Master Olivier the Devil. Thus Cromwell will say: 'I have Parliament in my bag and the king in my pocket,' or with the hand which signs the

35

death warrant of Charles I. he will smear with ink the face of a regicide who does the same to him laughingly. Thus Caesar in the triumphal chariot is afraid of upsetting; for men of genius however great they may be have in them an imp which parodies their intelligence. It is by this quality that they link themselves with humanity and it is by this that they are dramatic.

'From the sublime to the ridiculous is only one step,' said Napoleon when he was convicted of being human, and this flash from a fiery soul laid bare illumines at once art and history, this cry of anguish is the summing up of drama and of life."

That is superb eloquence. But the great poets are not always very exact thinkers. The question is badly put. We are not at all concerned to know whether in real life the ludicrous is mingled with the terrible; in other words, whether the course of human events furnishes by turns to those who are either spectators or participants food for laughter and for tears. That is the one truth which no one questions and which has never been questioned. But the point at issue is altogether different. Twelve hundred persons are gathered together in the same room and form an audience. Are these twelve hundred persons likely to pass easily from tears to laughter and from laughter to tears? Is the playwright capable of transporting the audience from the one impression to the other? And does he not run the risk of enfeebling both impressions by this sudden contrast?

For example, to confine ourselves to the historic incidents cited by Victor Hugo, it does not at all concern us to know whether Cromwell after having signed the death warrant of Charles I. did or did not smear with ink the face of one of his colleags; whether this coarse pleasantry did or did not give rise to a coarse laugh in the assembly. The fact is authentic; we do not attempt to question it. The only thing we ask (in dramatic art, at least) is whether the fact, if placed on the stage just as it happened, is likely to please the twelve hundred persons in the audience.

These twelve hundred persons are entirely occupied with the death of Charles I. concerning which the author has sought to stir their pity. They are shedding tears of sympathy and tenderness. Suddenly the author places before them an act of broad buffoonery, alleging that in reality the grotesque mingles artlessly with the tragic. Do they laugh? And if they laugh do they experience a genuine satisfaction? Does not this laughter spoil the grief to which they found pleasure in abandoning themselves?

IV.

It has often been remarkt that laughter persists long after the causes have ceased, just as tears continue to flow after the arrival of the good news which should have dried them immediately. The human soul is not flexible enough to pass readily from one extreme of sensation to the contrary one. These sudden jolts overwhelm it with painful confusion.

From this reflexion, of which no one, I believe, will dispute the justice, we may conclude that when a man is a prey to grief if he is diverted by an idea which inclines him to laughter, he is borne suddenly far from his sorrow and a certain lapse of time and a certain effort of will are necessary for him to return to it.

What is true of one man is even more true of a crowd. We have seen that the peculiar characteristic of an audience is that it feels more keenly than the individuals composing it. It enters more impetuously into the reasons for weeping that the poet gives it; the grief that it experiences is more intense, the tears are readier and more abundant.

I forget what tyrant it was of ancient Greece to whom massacres were every-day affairs, but who wept copiously over the misfortunes of a heroine in a tragedy. He was audience; and for the one evening clothed himself in the sentiments of the public.

It is also more difficult for an audience to return to an impression from which it has been diverted by an accident of some sort. How many performances have been interrupted, how many plays failed the first night, because of a ludicrous slip by an actor or a piquant jest shouted from the gallery. All the house bursts out laughing. At once it becomes impossible for it to recover its equilibrium. It is now launcht on another tack. The most touching scenes will be turned into ridicule. The play is lost.

In real life, this mixing of laughter and tears, this difficulty of returning to your grief after having left it, has no such disadvantage. As we have already said repeatedly; nature is indifferent and so also is life. You weep; it is well. You laugh afterwards, as you please. You laugh when you should weep; you weep when it would be better to laugh. That is your affair. You may weep with one eye and laugh with the other as the weeping and laughing Jean of the legend. It makes little difference to us.

In the theater it is not the same. The author who brings upon the stage the events of life and who naturally desires to make them interesting to his audience, must find means to heighten and render more vivid and more enduring the impression he wishes to create.

If his intention is to provoke laughter, he will be led by that alone to guard against every incident that might induce sadness in his audience; and if, on the other hand, his purpose is to compel tears, he will discard resolutely the circumstances which, by giving rise to laughter, might tend to counteract the emotion he wishes to arouse. He is not concerned in the least to know whether in reality laughter is mingled with tears. He does not seek to reproduce the truth, but to give the illusion of truth to the twelve hundred spectators:—a very different matter. When these twelve hundred spectators are entirely overwhelmed with grief they cannot believe that joy exists; they do not think about it; they do not wish to think about it; it displeases them when they are torn suddenly from their illusion in order to be shown another aspect of the same subject.

And if you do show it to them against their will, if you force them to change abruptly from tears to laughter, and this last impression once becomes dominant, they will cling to it and a return to the mood they have abandoned will be almost impossible. In life minutes are not counted, and we have all the time we need to bring about the transition from one sentiment to the other. But in the theater where we have at our disposal at most only four hours to exhibit all the series of events composing the action, the changes must take place swiftly and, so to speak, on the minute. This a man would resist if he were by himself; all the more will he resist it when he is one of a crowd.

To be strong and durable an impression

must be single. All dramatists have felt this instinctively; and it is for this reason that the distinction between the comic and the tragic is as old as art itself.

It would seem that when drama came into being the writers of ancient times would have been led to mingle laughter with tears, since drama represents life, and in life joy goes hand in hand with grief, the grotesque always accompanying the sublime. And yet the line of demarcation has been drawn from the beginning. It seems that, without realizing the philosophic reasons we have just set forth, the dramatic poets have felt that in order to sound the depths of the soul of the audience they must strike always at the same spot; that the impression would be stronger and more enduring in proportion as it was unified.

Do you find the least little word to excite laughter in the grand conceptions of Aeschylus or the simple and powerful dramas of Sophocles? It is true that in Sophocles the characters of humble condition express themselves in familiar language which may seem comic to those of us who have been nourisht in the tradition of a necessary dignity in tragedy. But this style has nothing of the comic in itself, no more, for example, than the chattering of the Nurse in Shakspere's 'Romeo and Juliet.'

These characters speak as they would speak naturally; but what they say does not alter in any way the impression of sadness that is to result from the whole. They do not give a turn to the events different from what the author intended. They do not divert the attention of the audience either to themselves or to ludicrous incidents. They contribute in the measure of their ability, with the qualities peculiar to their minds and their temperaments to the general impression. We hardly find except in Euripides, innovator and decadent genius, buffoonery deliberately mingled with drama, the grotesque invading tragedy. The drunken scene between Hercules and Admetus, who is mourning the death of Alcestis, is a celebrated example of this kind.

I need not say that with us more than with any other people this distinction of species has been markt from the beginning, until recent times. We have even carried it to the extreme, for we have an exaggerated love of logic.

In the 'Malade Imaginaire,' which is a comedy and which consequently should turn entirely on laughter, Argan stretches himself on his couch and pretends to be dead, and Angélique is told that she has lost her father. Angélique in tears throws herself beside her father whom she really believes to be dead. Suppose that Molière, forgetting that he was writing a comedy, had insisted on this situation, which after all is very touching. Suppose that he had prolonged it, that he had shown Angélique overcome with grief, ordering mourning, arranging for the funeral, and finally by dint of the tenderness exprest and the tears shed, wringing tears from the audience. He could have done it assuredly. It would not have been difficult for him to move the twelve hundred spectators with these displays of filial grief. And likewise in the scene in 'Tartuffe,' where Marianne kneels before her angry father to beg him to allow her to enter a convent.

If Molière had not restrained himself he might have committed the precise fault into which Shakspere, as I understand it, did not fall. He would have changed the aspect of events; I mean by this that he would have changed the mood in which he had led us to believe that the events would be treated. What was his intention? It was to show us, in contrast to Bélise punisht for her avarice, Angélique rewarded for her filial piety, and the audience roaring with laughter at the sight of her father raised from the dead to marry her to her lover.

It was an impression of gayety that he sought. He would have destroyed this impression had he dwelt too long on the grief of the young girl. From the same events he had meant to make use of in arousing laughter he could have extracted tears and the audience would no longer be in the mood for laughter at the proper moment. The shock would have been too strong for the transition to be made easily.

Try to recall your past theatrical experience; you will find that in all the melodramas, in all the tragedies, whether classic or romantic, into which the grotesque has crept, it has always been obliged to take an humble place, to play an episodic part; otherwise it would have destroyed the unity of impression which the author always strives to produce. Wherever this does not hold, it is because it was the secret design of the author to extract mirth from a situation which is sad in appearance. Thus in 'La Joie Fait Peur'; it is true that the situation in this play is that of a young man mourned by his mother, his *fiancée*, his sister, his friends, and his old servant. But the action is arranged in such a way that the entire audience is admitted at once to the secret that the young man is not dead. Everybody finally discovers this,— except the mother who remains disconsolate till the very end.

But who does not see that the joy of the others is one of the important elements in this amusing play, that it consequently occupies an important place in the mind of the audience and adds a certain mysterious savor of humor to the tears shed by the poor mother. The impression here then remains single, since far from being spoiled by the laughter which it arouses on its way the dramatic quality of the situation is really heightened. The principle is this: The impression must be single; any mingling of laughter and tears tends to destroy this. It is better therefore to avoid it. There is nothing more legitimate than the absolute distinction of the comic from the tragic, of the grotesque from the sublime. Yet nowadays every rule is subject to many exceptions. It is an exception when the playwright feels himself strong enough to subordinate particular impressions to the general impression, when he can so control the temper of his spectators as to turn them all at once from laughter to tears, when the public he is seeking to please is capable of passing easily from one attitude to another, because of its advanced civilization, its racial instincts, its prejudices due to its education.

It depends on whether the author believes himself able to subordinate the particular to the general impression which he wishes to produce, whether he is sufficiently master of the psychology of his audience to transport them by a single stroke from laughter to tears, and on whether the audience to which he addresses himself is, by reason of the state of civilization at which it has arrived, either by prejudice of education or instinct of race, likely to pass easily from one sentiment to the other.

The rule remains intact. The impression must be single; and it cannot be this if the characters brought in for the comic scenes are anything more than episodic, if their pleasantries are anything more than accessories which can be easily supported.

Nature itself and life are impartial in the presence of joy and sorrow, laughter and tears, and pass with perfect indifference from one sentiment to the other. But to have demonstrated this, as did Victor Hugo in the admirable passage which we cited above, proves nothing; since a play is not a reproduction of life but an aggregate of conventions designed to produce upon the spectators the illusion of life; and they cannot have this illusion if the author disconcerts them by changing the sentiments which he inspires, if he disarranges their pleasure.

V.

The conclusion is that the distinction between the comic and the tragic rests, not on a prejudice but on the very definition of drama; that this distinction may remain absolute without disadvantage; that there are disadvantages on the contrary if it is not observed; that nevertheless it may be disregarded—not without peril however—on this condition, that the disturbing element shall not interfere with the first impression which should remain single, and that it shall even heighten that impression by a slight effect of contrast.

Consider for a moment that we must come down to the middle of the eighteenth century to find in our literature a single comedy in which a situation turns toward the pathetic and is treated in a manner to bring tears to the eyes of the spectators.

There is no doubt that the founders of our drama, and above all the immortal Molière, had made the very simple observation that in life it often happens that the most joyful events face about suddenly and change joy into despair. After a good dinner you embark with some comrades in a boat for a fishing party. Your spirits are a little flusht with wine; somebody is guilty of an imprudence. A single person has preserved his good sense and warns you of the danger you are inviting. You laugh him to ridicule; he himself yields to the general hilarity. A puff of wind catches the boat crosswise; it capsizes; everybody falls into the water. Two or three remain there and are not recovered till the next day. Is there an accident of more common occurrence? It is the terrible and the pathetic breaking in abruptly and imposing silence on laughter and changing it to tears. This is seen every day; it is the regular course of life.

If the masters of the drama, who could not have failed to make so simple an observation, have nevertheless written as if it had been unknown to them, it is apparent that their sole purpose was not to exhibit life as it really is on the stage, that they had in view another object,—that of showing life in a certain aspect to twelve hundred persons assembled in a theater, and of producing on the multiple soul of this audience a certain impression.

They must have said to themselves, or rather they felt instinctively, that every sensation is stronger the more it is prolonged without being opposed by any other; that an individual, and still more an audience, does not pass easily from laughter to tears in order to return immediately from tears to laughter; that they cling to the first impression; that if you wrench them violently from one sentiment and throw them into a contrary, it will be almost impossible to bring them back later on; that these jolts threaten to destroy their pleasure for them, and are especially wrong because they give the impression that in the theater all is false, the events as well as the lighting, thus destroying the illusion.

As we do not pass in real life suddenly from laughter to tears and return immediately, or almost immediately, from tears to laughter, as the suddenness of these changes, however abrupt they may be, is relieved by intervals of time more or less considerable, which the authors cannot preserve in the theater, the rapidity of these movements, aside from the fact that they tire the audience, has this curious disadvantage, that in pretending to give us life in all its reality they destroy the illusion of this same reality.

You may search all Molière, all Regnard, all Dufresny, all Dancourt, and the rest of the dramatists of the beginning of the eighteenth century, without finding in them a scene which is not in the key suitable to comedy. If all the scenes are not comic, all at least are amiable and pleasant. You will find in them often tender conversations be-

tween lovers, scenes of jealousy, lovers opposed by parents; but these scenes present to
the mind only the agreeable images of youth
and hope. If there is mingled with them
some shadow of sadness, it is a grief which
is not without sweetness; the smile is always
just beneath the tears, as in that admirable
account of Hector's farewell to Andromache,
which remains the best example of these
mingled sentiments of sun and shower.

Molière never wrote, nor wisht to write,
anything but comedies which were comedies
from beginning to end. And if you will go
back to classic antiquity you will see that he
was not an innovator. Show me a passage
in Plautus to weep over; and even Terence
restricts himself to this scale of tempered
sentiments,—to scenes in which, if he allows
the tears sometimes to form on the eyelashes,
they never fall, and are wiped away at once
with a smile.

Everywhere the characteristic of comedy
in the great periods in which it flourisht is
to be comic.

And even to-day, look at the pieces truly
worthy of the name, from those of Augier to
the marvellous farces of the Palais-Royal by

Labiche, Meilhac, and Gondinet. Do you find in them any mixture of the pathetic? Is the unity of impression destroyed by a tearful scene? Can you easily imagine in 'Célimare le Bien-Aimé,' the 'Effrontés,' the 'Testament de César Girodot,' the 'Faux-Bonshommes,' the 'Gendre de M. Poirier,' or 'Mercadet' a situation which brings tears to the eyes?

I have here chosen purposely as examples works very diverse in tone and in style in order to show that this great law of the unity of impression—without which there is no possibility of illusion for an audience of twelve hundred persons—has been observed instinctively by all the playwrights who were truly endowed with the comic genius.

NOTES

NOTES

FRANCISQUE SARCEY (1827-1899) was a graduate of the Ecole Normale, having as classmates, Taine, Edmond About and Prévost-Paradol. In his 'Souvenirs de Jeunesse' (1884), of which there is a translation in English, he has left an amusing account of his student years. Upon his graduation he was duly appointed as a professor of French literature in one of the smaller cities of France. Those were the most dismal and depressing days of the Second Empire; and Sarcey's frankness in expressing his liberal opinions rendered it certain that he could not hope for promotion. In 1858 Edmond About persuaded him to drop teaching for journalism, —just as Jules Lemaitre was to do a quarter of a century later.

At first Sarcey was a journalistic free lance, writing in all the periodicals, daily or weekly, which he could persuade to accept his articles and writing on all sorts of subjects, literary and linguistic, social and political. It was only after several years of this miscellaneous newspaper hackwork, that he began to specialize as a theatrical reviewer; and he attracted little attention until 1867 when he was appointed dramatic critic of the *Temps*, then as now the most reputable and the most dignified of Parisian dailies. Thereafter for forty-two years he contributed to the *Temps* every Sunday afternoon a dramatic criticism, which came speedily to possess an indisputable authority.

In 1878 he began a series of studies of the actors and actresses of the Comédie-Française and of the other important theaters of Paris,—'Comédiens et Comédiennes.' He continued to contribute to various newspapers articles on topics of contemporary interest, social and political. He became a frequent lecturer; and in his 'Souvenirs d'Age Mur' (1892), also translated into English, he analized with his characteristic acuteness the principles of public speaking. He refused regretfully an invitation to become a member of the French Academy, fearing that he would not be free to express his opinions frankly and fully. He declined also the cross of the Legion of Honor; and he declared that all he wanted upon his tombstone was the record that he had been both "Professor and Journalist."

At the beginning of the first volume of 'Quarante Ans de Théâtre,' the editor printed a selection from the many warmly appreciative articles which appeared in the French press immediately after Sarcey's death in 1899. Noteworthy among these were the tributes of Jules Claretie, Jules Lemaitre and Emile Faguet. Jules Lemaitre had earlier publisht in the second volume of his 'Contemporains' a characteristically clever study of Sarcey. The article by Henry James, (to which reference is made in the Intioduction) is entitled the 'Théâtre Français'; and it is included in his volume on 'French Poets and Novelists' (1878).

The essential point of Sarcey's attempt to formulate a theory of the theater is that all the laws of the drama are the result of the fact that every play is intended to be performed before an audience and that therefore the desires, the opinions, and the prejudices of the spectators must always be taken into account. No one has declared this undeniable truth so completely as Sarcey. Yet other French critics have set forth similar views. In his lectures on the 'Epochs of the French Theater' Ferdinand Brunetière pointed out that altho men of letters in France between 1550 and 1600 were trying to write plays, there were then no professional actors, no regular theater, and therefore no public before which plays could be performed:—"Now a play does not begin to exist as a play except before the footlights, by virtue of the collaboration and of the complicity of the public, without which a play never has been, and never can be, anything more than a mere literary exercise."

In Jules Lemaitre's 'Corneille et la Poétique d'Aristote' there is an account of the vain struggles of Corneille against the rigors of the classicist code which the Italian critics had elaborated from their misreading of Aristotle; and Lemaitre quoted Corneille's plea for permission to employ a neutral ground, not specifically anywhere, in which all the characters of a tragedy might be supposed to meet. Corneille defined this as a "theatrical fiction," akin to the legal fictions accepted by lawyers; and Lemaitre commented that the theatrical fictions which Corneille askt the privilege of using are simply what we now know as the conventions of the drama :—

"If the characters of tragedy speak in verse,—that is a convention. If they meet every time they have something to say to one another,—that is a convention. If they talk aloud when they are alone,—that is a convention. If the poet develops under our eves a single action, altho there are none in real life not tangled up with a host of others, —that is a convention. He who seeks to abolish conventions can only change them. The alleged Rules of the unity of Time and the unity of Place, had for their purpose, as Corneille admits, to suppress certain conventions, which were, however, easily acceptable; and then, to obey these Rules, Corneille invents conventions of his own, far less simple and far more difficult to accept,' (pp. 67-68).

In the preface to his 'Etrangère,' the younger Dumas with his customary incisiveness lends his support to Sarcey, altho without mentioning him:—"In all the arts there is a share, larger or smaller but indispensable, which must be left to convention. Sculpture lacks color; painting lacks relief; and they are rarely, either the one or the other, of the dimensions of the object they represent. The more richly you bestow on a statue the colors of life, the more surely you inflict upon it the appearance of death, because in the definitive attitude to which it is condemned by its material, it must lack movement—and movement even more than color and form is the proof of life. . . . Nature is the basis, the means of art, it is not the aim of art. . . . Whether he wields the mallet, the pen or the brush, the artist really merits the name only when he can give a soul to the things of matter and a form to the things of the soul, when, in a word, he idealizes the real he sees and realizes the ideal he feels."

B. M.

OF THIS BOOK THREE HUNDRED AND
THIRTY-THREE COPIES WERE PRINTED
FROM TYPE BY CORLIES, MACY AND
COMPANY IN SEPTEMBER : MCMXVI

Bei Fragen zur Produktsicherheit wenden Sie sich bitte an:
If you have any questions regarding product safety,
please contact:

Walter de Gruyter GmbH
Genthiner Straße 13
10785 Berlin
productsafety@degruyterbrill.com